CELEBRATING QUIET PEOPLE

Uplifting Stories

for

Introverts

and

Highly Sensitive Persons

Prasenjeet Kumar

Copyright Prasenjeet Kumar 2015

All rights reserved. No part of this book may be reproduced, stored in a retrieval system, or transmitted, in any form or by any means, electronic, mechanical, photocopying, recording or otherwise, without the prior permission of the copyright owner, accept in the case of brief quotations embodied in critical articles or reviews.

Cover credit: Jim Kukral, Author Marketing Club

The spellings used in this book are British, which may look strange to my American friends, but NOT to those living in Australia, Canada, India, Ireland and of course the United Kingdom. This means that color is written as colour and so on. I hope that is NOT too confusing!

Your FREE Gift

As a way of saying thanks for your purchase, I'm offering FREE the first few chapters of my first book in the Quiet Phoenix series i.e. "**Quiet Phoenix: An Introvert's Guide to Rising in Career & Life**". The book has been on the Amazon #1 Best Seller list in Legal Profession and Ethics and Professional Responsibility.

You can download the sample chapters by going here:

http://eepurl.com/_-WU

Table of Contents

Are Introverts Underperformers? 5

    True Story of an Introvert whose rich Imagination took her to Phenomenal Success: 7

    A Tongue Tied Law Student Defeats his more Eloquent Colleagues in Mooting: 13

    Abraham Lincoln used his introversion as a strength to become the greatest leader of all times 27

Standing Up to Bullies-the Quiet Way 35

    A Trainee stands up to his Bully Boss in a Corporate Law World: 37

    A Quiet Girl Teaches Bullies A Lesson in Her Own Quiet Way: 53

    A "Quiet dull witted child" becomes an immortal scientist: 59

Lessons that all Introvert Entrepreneurs can Learn: 65

Living Your Dreams: 71

Which is more important: Happiness and Love or Money and Stress? 73

A Big Thank You! 77

FREE GIFT: 79

Do You Also Want To Write A Book? 81

Acknowledgment: 83

Disclaimer: 85

Other Books by the Author: 87

Books By The Author in Other Genres: 93

Connect with Me: 103

About the Author: 105

A Letter from a Quiet Revolutionary

Dear Reader,

First of all, let me thank you for picking this book up from a million others and deciding to invest your precious time to read it.

This book is written to celebrate the unique characteristics of quiet, introverts and highly sensitive persons.

But why should anyone write about such persons, you may wonder.

So let me explain.

Introverts and highly sensitive persons are often at a disadvantage in society. Parents, teachers, co-workers and bosses wonder why they are not assertive, open to sharing, not sociable enough, shy or in general lack the will to fight back. They are accused of not being team players. And bullies (both in school and in the work place) think they are easy pushovers.

Still no one should assert that introverts do not have any strengths. After all, many eminent personalities like Abraham Lincoln, Albert Einstein, Walt Disney, and even J.K. Rowling were introverts.

In fact, reading a lot of psychology books (including Susan Cain's Quiet the power of introverts in a world that can't stop talking) made me realise of my own unique potential, and my powers (or super powers, as I might say) that only a few years back I was not very conscious of.

This resulted into the writing of the Quiet Phoenix series. The theme of the series was that just as the Phoenix bird has the potential to be reborn literally from the ashes, so do introverts have the power to rise from any difficult situation.

Let's use a formula to understand this:

Quiet (introverts or highly sensitive persons)

+

Phoenix (or the ability to rise from the ashes)

=

Quiet Phoenix

This book contains 8 short stories based on the very same theme of Quiet Phoenix. I have tried to make these as interesting and readable as possible. It is indeed my endeavour to NOT make any of my books in this series sound like dull psychology textbooks.

So sorry to disappoint, therefore, if you are looking for some high-sounding, half-baked, pseudo-psychological mumbo-jumbo.

All stories are deeply motivating and inspirational. They tell us about how these really famous introverts overcame, with steely resolve, the most difficult challenges thrown their way. Above all, these stories highlight the importance of hard work, persistence, self-discipline, and having a vision or a rich imagination which all Quiet persons are fortunately, naturally endowed with.

I sincerely hope that these stories will give you too the courage to pursue your dreams and ambitions, regardless of how "outlandish" they may seem to others.

I wish you all the best with a pleasurable reading experience!

Regards,

Prasenjeet Kumar

I

Are Introverts Underperformers?

Most societies, whether Western or Eastern, value extroversion as an ideal self. "Successful" personalities are considered to be 'bold, assertive, those who can take the centre stage and a fellow who is mighty likeable'.

Introverts are often misunderstood. At home, parents worry if their quiet child is spending too much time in solitude, day dreaming whereas the real world operates through socialising and networking. At school, teachers presume that if a child is hesitant in answering questions, that child must be displaying some kind of learning or social disability. At work, introverts are considered to be not good 'team players' and lacking in enthusiasm and initiative.

In this part, I present a few short stories to dispel this myth; and to re-emphasise that introverts are gifted with the strengths of persistence, hard work, creativity, self-discipline, a knack for self-learning, high emotional intelligence and a rich imagination.

Can you believe that some the most famous personalities of the world were introverts? Not sure. Then browse through the next few pages to find out more.

1

True Story of an Introvert whose rich Imagination took her to Phenomenal Success

Joanne loved reading fantasy books as a little girl and even tried writing some short stories. Like a typical introvert, she had a rich imagination. Wizards, magic and sorcery formed part of her world. She thought she should be a novelist. But she came from an impoverished background. Her parents wanted to her to do a vocational course---a course that would empower her to secure a real job in the real world.

"Your overactive imagination is good for amusing people but not enough to pay for a mortgage or for securing a pension, my little girl," her parents told her.

Joanne's parents were being practical. After all, there is nothing noble about poverty.

Joanne loved her fantasy world. That universe was a part of her. Leaving that world was as traumatic as separating from your loved and dear ones.

In the university, Joanne's parents wanted her to do a "useful" course while she wanted to study English literature. Joanne did not want to upset her parents. So she agreed to pursue a degree in modern languages. However, at the last moment, she enrolled herself in a course in Classics not informing her parents about her sudden change in decision.

University life was a different world altogether. A world where students were busy attending lectures, seminars and preparing for tutorials. Some worried about their careers after graduation. Some were simply partying and having fun. But Joanne was spending her time mostly in coffee bars writing stories and sometimes not even attending lectures. She was lucky to pass her exams.

In her mid-20s, she took up secretarial jobs. Then she got married and had a daughter. During lunch sessions, her writing bug did not leave her. Her employers noticed that Joanne was not paying attention to work. As a result, she lost her job numerous times.

Sadly, Joanne also had a failed marriage. Her world was crashing down all around her. There seemed no hope. She was miserably alone with an exceptionally short-lived marriage, jobless, a lone parent with a daughter to look after, and as poor as it was possible to be in modern Britain, "without being homeless." The fears that her parents nursed about her, and that she had for herself, had come true. She felt as if she was the biggest failure from any standard.

Joanne even contemplated suicide. There seemed nothing to look forward to in this world.

However, her daughter was something that made her come down to earth. Abandoning her for escaping from this world was definitely not the right thing to do.

Joanne decided to take full control of her life. A lack of success had taught her things that she never knew about herself. Failure made her discover her true self. It gave her an inner security which did not come from passing university examinations. Joanne realised that she had a stronger will and more discipline than she ever thought she had, which are also classic strengths of an introvert. Plus she had an old type writer and a story to tell to the world.

Joanne stopped believing that she could do nothing better than make a living out of a day job. She stopped suppressing her creative self which was supposedly of no use in the 'real world'.

One day on a train journey from London to Manchester and back, Joanne created a story of a boy wizard in her mind. She thought that to be a good bed time story for her daughter. Joanne had a pen that did not function and she was too shy to ask for one.

It was years later when she got down to writing that entire story, spending most of her time in a coffee shop. The owners did not want her to spend the whole day writing in long hand while ordering only one cup of coffee. But Joanne ignored the disapproving glances and plodded on.

A few years down the line, Joanne finished her manuscript. She had written 700 pages in long hand and then manually typed it. She now had to send the manuscript to publishers.

"Children's stories have no market," she was told straight to her face. Her manuscript was rejected one after another by twelve publishers. It was very easy to give up at that juncture. Joanne had never had any success in life. It seemed as if her entire life was jinxed.

Yet Joanne persisted. She sent her manuscript to the 13th publisher.

After a year, her wizard story finally found a home at Bloomsbury. She was granted a miserly $1500 advance. Her publisher advised her to keep her day job, as there just wasn't enough money in "children's literature," as they had all said.

The first printing of her book had a run of 1,000 copies, 500 of which were sent to libraries. Today, those original 1,000 books are worth $16,000 to $25,000 each. In early 1998, an auction was held in the U.S. for the rights to publish the book. Scholastic Inc won and paid Joanne $105,000. The book was published in the U.S. The money from the U.S. sales enabled Joanne and her daughter to move into a new home.

Her book attracted millions of fans from the world over, irrespective of culture or nationality, children or adult. She became the first person to become a billionaire from her books.

In 2006, Joanne released the seventh and the final book in the series that sold more than 400 million books worldwide. Her books have been translated into 65 different languages.

Joanne's patience, persistence and an unshakeable belief in herself more than paid off in the end. She is now happily married and has a son and a daughter.

Yes, you guessed it right.

I am indeed talking about the famous **J.K. Rowling**. Her first book, a boy wizard story, was **Harry Potter and the Philosopher's Stone**. Today, the Harry Potter brand, along with its movie franchisee, is worth billions of dollars.

In an article, J.K. Rowling thanked her introversion for the creation of the Harry Potter series.

You may like to read that article here: http://www.elle.com/life-love/introverted-women

Food for thought: Did you know that introverts are supposed to be more persistent and patient than their extrovert counterparts, especially when the going gets bumpy?

2

A Tongue Tied Law Student Defeats his more Eloquent Colleagues in Mooting

John was a quiet 17 year-old who had just passed out of High School. He had the dreams of becoming a lawyer.

In school, John was just too shy and hesitant to participate in debates. But John loved watching debates. He would often be surprised to find how his peers in school were so eloquent that they could literally answer any question on the spot without batting an eyelid or could defend any seemingly untenable position with grace.

John on the other hand was slow to gather his thoughts. Yet, John loved courtroom drama and always fantasised to be the centre of all attraction. It was this fantasy that led John to join the University

College London (UCL), Faculty of Laws, one of the most prestigious Law Colleges in the whole of the United Kingdom. John had good grades in high school and an amazing ability for logical reasoning which led him to pass the LNAT (The Law National Aptitude Test), just like the LSAT in the U.S., with comfortable ease.

UCL was a dream come true for John. The University had a reputation for producing fantastic 'mooters' who regularly won all national and international mooting competitions. Mooting is a mock courtroom situation where law students argue a fictitious case in front of a "judge."

Students are evaluated on the basis of eloquence, their ability to present arguments and most importantly on courtroom etiquette! This also, rather ludicrously, meant that students addressed the judge as "Your Lordship/Ladyship" or "My Lord/Lady" (this is British courtroom etiquette) than simply as "you" (remember the judge is not your friend).

The Junior Mooting Competition was always held every year at the beginning of the new term session so that First year students could get a grasp of what mooting is like before they jumped in. John too joined in to watch the Final Mooting round.

There were four students all of them looking nervous. The judge in the Final round was a real judge meaning that he was an actual district court level judge. To say the judge was nasty would be quite an

;understatement. He used to literally fire a lot of questions, most of them being incomprehensible. He ripped and trashed all arguments presented by reasonably competent law students. He made some students speak exceptionally fast and some to stammer and stutter. For John, the experience was both scary and exciting.

After the Mooting Competition was over and winners announced, First year students were asked to sign up for the Junior Mooting Competition. The sign up list was put up in the main corridor of Bentham House, which is another name for UCL's Law School. The School was named after Jeremy Bentham, the famous Utilitarian Philosopher, a Lawyer and founder of UCL.

John slowly moved towards the corridor. Some students looked excited while others looked a little nervous. There was a tussle going on inside John's mind.

"I'm not a good speaker. I am slow to gather my thoughts. Plus I have never participated in public speaking. I don't have the necessary experience."

"No Wait, John. This is your chance to prove yourself wrong. You have a good ability for logical reasoning. Why not give it a try?"

"And what make a fool of myself publicly?"

"Why think this way? Why don't you think that you can impress the judges and your colleagues? After all you often fantasise about taking the centre stage. This could be the chance you were looking for. Don't be a sissy!"

"I'm not a sissy! To hell with you."

John took out his pen and with his hands trembling a bit, he wrote his name down on the sign up list. After signing up, John was provided a random sheet of paper with the fictitious case he was supposed to argue.

John picked up the piece of paper to read. He couldn't believe what he just saw.

"Bill and Chris were great friends. One evening both of them decided to visit the Blue Ox pub. On the way back, Chris asked for a lift from Bill as Bill knew the road in the dark. Bill agreed. While driving on the road, Bill started seeing pink cats on the road. Fearing that he might hit the pink cats, Bill swerved suddenly on a clear level stretch and hit the divider. The car came to a rest at the middle of the carriageway. Chris immediately jumped out of the window and suffered crippling injuries. A truck was coming from the opposite direction. Both vehicles collided. Bill too suffered injuries and had to be taken to the hospital. Chris decided to sue Bill for negligent drunk driving. The lower court awarded the damages in favour of Chris and now Bill appeals in the Court of Appeal."

John was supposed to argue in favour of Bill, the "drunk driver."

"This seems like an open and shut case!" John thought to himself.

"How can anyone possibly defend a driver guilty of drinking and putting his friend's life in danger?"

John was given 15 days to prepare for the mock court. Skeleton arguments had to be submitted to the judges a day before the mock courtroom trial.

John wanted to pull back desperately but it was too late. Then a voice in his head spoke to him:

"Persuade yourself first that Bill is not guilty before convincing others."

Following this voice, John decided to accept the challenge. He could overhear his other colleagues bragging that the fictitious case was a cheese cake as they were representing Chris, the poor guy who fractured his fingers.

Every evening after finishing his lectures, John sat in the Law Library for hours pondering over cases and cases. Nothing seemed to be supporting him. All the cases stated only one thing that the driver owes a 'duty of care' to its passenger; meaning that it is the responsibility of the driver to ensure that the passenger in his care is safe at all times.

"What arguments can I possibly come up with?" John kept on wondering.

"That it was alright to get drunk or to party but I may sound like a fool!"

"Any public policy arguments...?"

"My Lords, you should not award damages in favour of Chris because doing so would paralyse the beer and whisky industry something which Brits are so fond of...."

"What the heck is wrong with you, John. That is the stupidest argument I have ever heard," John said to himself.

Days were passing by and John's frustration was growing.

"There has to be a way," John tried to exhort himself.

There was now only one day left before the mock court session. Skeleton arguments had to be submitted to the judges via e-mail.

Yes, judges! This was a Court of Appeal trial which meant that there were going to be as many as three judges presiding over the mock court trial.

Three judges! John was scared of one but now there were going to be three firing all sorts of questions making John look like a complete idiot.

John as usual was pondering over case law sitting in the Law Library. He was exhausted but not willing to give up. In the previous 14 days, he had read a lot, much more than his counterparts.

John got up from his seat to find another Law Report and accidentally dropped one on the floor. When he picked up that Law Report to put it back on the shelf, he saw that there was a case which dealt with a matter within his area of law.

John started reading the case curiously. His eyes lit up a little.

"May be this case could be of some importance to me but I am not sure."

John re-read the fictitious case again. He was surprised to find an important piece of fact that he had completely overlooked. A piece of fact that could save John's fictitious client.

John went back to his seat and started sketching out his skeleton argument. He was done in an hour and quickly e-mailed his argument to the judges from one of the Library computers.

He rushed back to his student Hall of Residence. Now came the speech preparation bit. John's fear of public speaking came back to haunt him.

"I'm not as eloquent as my other peers," John was mired in self-doubt.

However, John knew that instead he was gifted with the powers of preparation and perspiration, a power he could almost unconsciously exercise. John returned to his room at 8:30 in the evening. He had to do something about his speech preparation.

John first wrote down all his arguments on a piece of paper in long hand. He then stood in front of a mirror holding that piece and started to rehearse the way actors do.

At first, John felt awkward. Speaking to yourself in front of a mirror was not a very pleasing experience.

"Mmmmmayyy it please your Lordships..." John stuttered.

He didn't like hearing his own voice which was far from perfect. John realised that he was nervous and was stammering quite a bit. He could not give this impression to the judges in the Moot Court session.

John persisted. With every effort, his voice became better and more confident. He rehearsed his argument so many times that he memorised it. He kept on improvising his delivery till it sounded presentable to him. Tired and stressed out, John finally crashed into the bed at 2:30 a.m. in the morning. Tomorrow was going to be a long day for him.

The Moot Court session was to commence at 7 p.m. the next day. John reached the Moot courtroom at 5:30 p.m. dressed in a black suit and a red tie. This was the second time John had been to the Moot Court room.

The room seemed magnificent like a typical courtroom with reddish brown leather seats, wood panelled walls and chandeliers hanging from the ceiling. The dais, where the judges would sit, was placed on an elevation so that they could look down upon everyone else with haughty disdain.

Slowly everyone started pouring in, including John's colleague arguing for the opposite party and the Court clerk. Everyone took their seats and organised their papers. The judges entered the courtroom exactly at 7 p.m. When the Court clerk announced "All rise," everyone stood up.

The judges started with the claimant first which in this case was John's colleague. The judges looked extremely bored with life. John was only thankful that he was not the one who was speaking first. John's opponent introduced himself and John first, explained the brief facts of the case and what the law was and after that started putting forward his arguments (called submissions).

John had rightly anticipated his opponent's arguments. His 'Learned Friend' made the standard 'duty of care' argument that his client (Chris) suffered injuries due to Bill's negligent driving and that as a driver of the vehicle, it was Bill's responsibility to ensure Chris' safety.

The judges nodded in agreement. John's 'Learned Friend' had done a good job of making the case sound like a simple open and shut scenario.

Now, it was John's responsibility to cast doubts over a case which sounded so one sided. John got up to speak, with butterflies in his stomach.

"My Lords, my Client Bill is not liable to pay damages. This is because my Learned Friend's Client, Chris, suffered crippling injuries because he decided to jump out of the car in sheer panic. Had he not done so, he would not have suffered those injuries," John said.

"Mr. John, have you forgotten that Chris anticipated a collision coming from a truck from the opposite side?" Intervened one of the judges quite harshly.

"Your Lordships have a point but the facts do not say that Chris expected a collision. In fact, the car had just come to a halt in the middle of the carriageway. It is not clear that Chris perceived an imminent danger before acting in sheer panic. This means that Chris could have avoided those injuries had he not panicked and jumped out of the window," John persisted.

The judges took a pause and read the facts again. They looked a bit puzzled.

"Mr. John that is a very weak argument. Chris suffered crippling injuries due to your Client's misconduct. Chris was acting reasonably and with caution when he decided to take a dangerous leap to avoid the collision," said one of the judges.

At this moment, John realised why the judges were so hesitant in accepting his arguments. No legal system in the world would take drunk driving so lightly. So, John decided to take a different approach.

"My Lords, Chris and my Client were very good friends. Both had visited the pub together. This means that Chris knew very well that my Client could get drunk, yet he accepted the ride," John argued.

The judges looked a little intrigued and started looking at the facts again.

"My Lords, this means that Chris accepted the obvious risk of injury. He could have very easily taken a cab back home, which is something that all reasonable men do after having a pint or two of beer." John said.

The judges and the opponents were listening very carefully.

"Mr. John, what are you trying to prove?" queried a judge.

"This means my Lords that my Learned Friend's Client was not acting responsibly. He first made my Client drunk and then accepted a lift from him knowing very well that he was drunk. My Learned Friend's Client was thus solely responsible for putting his own life at risk," John said.

"Mr. John, do you have any case law supporting your claim", the judges now wanted to conclude.

"Yes, my Lords," said John and he took out a copy of the case that he had accidentally glanced through when a Law Report had fallen on the ground.

John handed over a copy of the judgement to the judges and asked them to turn to page six. The judges adjusted their spectacles to read.

"Would your Lordships like a brief summary of the facts of case?" asked John.

"Yes, please," said the judges.

"In this case, a man agreed to be flown by the pilot in his light aircraft knowing very well that the pilot was drunk. Shortly after take-off the aircraft crashed and the pilot was killed. The man was severely injured and decided to sue the dead pilot. His claims were rejected by the same court on the grounds that the man knew that the pilot was drunk. The man, therefore, accepted the full risk of serious injury himself. The pilot was considered not negligent, my Lords," John said.

"My Lords, the facts in the present case are not very different from this judgment. The same rule should apply," John added.

The judges looked at the document and then looked at John surprised.

"Very well, Mr. John. Now we need some time to consider the matter. The court is dismissed," the judges said and retreated to the chamber adjoining the court room.

There was a lot of excitement. Who was going to win and who was going to lose that night?

After ten minutes, the judges came back to the moot court room.

"After carefully listening to all of the submissions made by both parties, and strictly going by the law, we have come to the conclusion that Bill was NOT negligent," the judges announced their verdict.

John's face lit up. His opponent looked surprised and crestfallen.

The judges in their feedback told John that his performance was the best they had ever heard in a long time. John's meticulous preparation and perspiration had obviously paid off. He had read extensively about the subject matter and anticipated all of his opponent's arguments.

A shy, tongue tied law student had just used his gifts of introversion (i.e. of extensive preparation) to go on to win the Junior Mooting Competition.

"Anyone can achieve their fullest potential, who we are might be predetermined, but the path we follow is always of our own choosing. We should never allow our fears or the expectations of others to set

the frontiers of our destiny. Your destiny can't be changed but, it can be challenged..."

– **Martin Heidegger**

(This true story is based on my own mooting experience in UCL where I had the privilege to study Law from 2005-2008 leading to my LLB (Honours) degree.)

3

Abraham Lincoln used his introversion as a strength to become the greatest leader of all times

In Corporate Management, it is always taught that leaders should be "bold," "assertive," "charismatic," and "pounding the table" types who have the ability to carry the crowd with them. There is also a lurking misconception that introverts i.e. those who speak softly, who are drained by social meetings and who work quietly, cannot be effective leaders.

History proves otherwise. Introverts have some special gifts which if they use well, can make them become as effective as, or in some cases even outperform, their extroverted counterparts.

Abraham Lincoln is the prime example of how introverts can utilise their inner strengths to become the greatest leader of all times.

Lincoln was born in abject poverty. His father barely had the ability to read and write. His mother was only a little better. So Lincoln had learnt reading and writing from his mother.

Lincoln was struck with tragedy after tragedy. His mother died due to milk sickness (a disease which was prevalent in 19th century America and occurred due to the poisoning of cow's milk after the cow ate snakeroot), when he was only a young boy. Lincoln lost his brother and sister too when he was young.

It is said that introverts are hard-wired to be more persistent than their extrovert counterparts and Lincoln was the perfect example. His story of failures is well known and is often repeated to motivate others to never give up. Lincoln lost a job, failed in business twice, was defeated in elections eight times, became bankrupt and incurred a debt which took nearly seventeen years to be repaid, suffered a nervous breakdown and was bed ridden for six months. And he had to deal with the loss of the woman he deeply loved (Anne Rutledge).

The list of his failures do not end here and if I were to list all of them, I am sure they would run into pages. Yet the biggest lesson one can learn is that Abraham Lincoln never quit. He could have very easily considered himself "unlucky" or that he was destined to fail.

But Lincoln did not let his destiny dictate him; instead he dictated his own destiny to become the greatest President that America ever saw.

However, there was more to Lincoln than his "never give up" attitude. In nature, he was modest and humble. Since his younger days, Lincoln was described as *"easy-going," "smiling," "tender and warm," "simple and sincere,"* and *"pure,"* all qualities that come very naturally to introverts.

Lincoln was the man '*who did not offend by superiority,*' as Ralph Waldo Emerson once wrote. In other words, Lincoln did not act authoritarian, bossy or considered his peers and subordinates as pests. Speaker of the House, Schuyler Colfax, once remarked, *"No man clothed with such vast power ever wielded it more tenderly and forbearingly."* With his modest personality, Lincoln could win over everyone-friends, adversaries, allies, enemies or the common folk.

Lincoln was also empathetic and compassionate, another gift of introversion. Some have said that Lincoln's tough childhood made him more sensitive towards others. It is true that Lincoln like any other human being had severe bouts of depression but he channelised his depression into compassion and love for others.

During war times, he travelled long distances to visit soldiers on the battlefield. In this way, he earned the respect and unmitigated support of the soldiers who felt that there was someone who acknowledged their contribution and sacrifice. One soldier even wrote a letter to his family members saying, *"Lincoln's warm smile was a reflection of his honest, kindly heart; but deeper, under the surface of that...were the unmistakable signs of care."*

Despite so much of bitterness all-around, Lincoln never vilified the Southerners for practising slavery, something that Lincoln was personally very much against. The famous quote *"They (Southerners) are just what we would be in their situation. If slavery did not now exist amongst them, they would not introduce it. If it did now exist amongst us, we should not instantly give it up..."* exemplifies his empathy towards Southerners.

So it becomes obvious that a great leader must have empathy towards his employees, peers and adversaries if he is to succeed.

Introverts have a knack for self-learning and so did Lincoln. He was his own guru. Born in poverty, Lincoln had very little formal schooling. Yet that did not prevent him from acquiring education. Other children used to practice writing on paper but there was no paper in Abraham's house. So he practised writing and math at the back of a wooden spoon using charcoal as pencil.

Lincoln mastered grammar, language and expression all by himself. He learnt maths including geometry and trigonometry all on his own. He practised public speaking in front of his friends and diligently studied Shakespeare. He even once told a student *"always bear in mind that your own resolution to succeed is more important than any one thing."*

During his lawyer days, Lincoln would meet up with his friends in the evening and engage in story-telling contests. He also learnt the trades of boatman, merchant, clerk, postmaster, surveyor and country lawyer before being elected as a U.S. Congressman in his thirties. He has been described to be a self-taught lawyer who read and re-read Blackstone's Commentaries till he understood them thoroughly.

Author Jennifer Kahnweiler even calls Abraham Lincoln a "geek" meaning someone who possessed deep knowledge about a subject. Lincoln was the most sought Patent and Copyright lawyer in Illinois. He even had deep knowledge about voting behaviour. i.e. he had a firm grasp of voting patterns, turnouts, and trends.

No wonder Abraham Lincoln was one of the greatest leaders to walk on this Earth. If you have to become a leader in your organisation, commit yourself to a life of self-discipline and self-learning. Again, introverts have an edge here over their extrovert counterparts.

Introverts are considered to be more receptive of ideas. They are approachable and are considered more willing to hear and implement new suggestions than extroverts who usually lead by *"putting their own stamp."* This was true about Abraham Lincoln.

He was regarded as a master listener who listened to conflicting views and oppositions. People were free to disagree with him without apprehending any form of retaliation. Lincoln encouraged an atmosphere of open dialogue which was necessary during the Civil War. Executives too can model their behaviour on Lincoln and this is where introverts can simply work on their strengths and gain inspiration from Lincoln.

Abraham Lincoln was also passionate about his work. He had a clear vision. He sincerely believed that he had a purpose to fulfil. *"Every man is said to have his peculiar ambition,"* he wrote once. *"I have no other so great as that of being truly esteemed by fellow men, by rendering myself worthy of their esteem."*

Lincoln acted out of this deep commitment and passion for his work rather than showing his might as the President of the United States. His lifelong motivation was to eradicate slavery completely from his country once and for all. Lincoln could convince others only because he believed in his own noble cause himself. He was not after power or money.

"His speaking went to the heart because it came from the heart," reported Horace White. Lincoln's compassion for others made him stand out as a great

benevolent leader. It has also been observed that like Lincoln introverts too perform better if they truly care about a subject than the possibility of any other reward in the shape of power or money.

In Corporate sessions, introverts are often criticised for being slow in taking decisions and for thinking through before they act. But Lincoln too was a thoughtful person. He never took any rash decisions. He genuinely believed that *"in order to win a man to your cause, you must first reach his heart, the great high road to his reason."* On many occasions he used to tell stories to soften feelings and dispel anxieties. Lincoln acted out of his conscience. This is why his audience could connect with him so deeply.

Enough proof to support that introverts can be gifted leaders.

"That some achieve great success, is proof to all that others can achieve it as well."

--Abraham Lincoln

II

Standing Up to Bullies-the Quiet Way

Bullies come in all forms, shapes and sizes. They are not only limited to schools but may be present in the workplace, in the relationship between spouses, among "friends", in fact, almost anywhere. It is often said that bullies usually pick on quiet persons because of the belief that such quiet or sensitive person would not have the courage or the will to fight back.

One way to deal with bullying is to learn to act equally aggressively. However, we present you a few short stories where two quiet people in different circumstances did not use aggression to pacify their bullies.

Instead they drew their strengths from their quiet personalities.

4

A Trainee stands up to his Bully Boss in a Corporate Law World

PK was a young, quiet, hardworking and highly enthusiastic Associate in a corporate law firm in Delhi. His work was consistently of high quality and many of his bosses and colleagues appreciated his work ethics deeply.

One day, he was asked to assist Mr. Black Horse, a Senior Associate (and technically PK's senior), from the Mumbai office of the same firm. Mr. Black Horse had come to work on a corporate transaction to Delhi.

A slightly tall guy around 5 feet 10 inches in height, Mr. Black Horse wore rimmed glasses. His arms and legs were skinny and un-athletic. He had developed a sizeable paunch which was quite revealing when he wore a T-shirt on Saturdays, a time when office colleagues used to dress down. In casual conversations, he always spoke about joining the gym (a typical non-serious corporate gossip) but given his disproportionate physique, it didn't look like he had exercised ever. Mr. Black Horse was quite enjoying the fat pay cheques and the Pepperoni Pizzas, in short, the luxuries of the Corporate World.

At first glance, Mr. Black Horse came across as a mild, friendly and occasionally humorous person. On the first day, he took PK out for a lunch and didn't let PK pay for his share of the meal.

"Our office will take care of it, don't worry!" Mr. Black Horse said with a grin.

During the lunch session, Mr. Black Horse told PK that he was originally from Delhi and his family members still lived in Delhi.

"It feels so great to be back home. I miss my family dearly," Mr. Black Horse said.

"Then why don't you work in Delhi?" PK asked.

"Huh.." Mr. Black Horse snorted at the stupidity inherent in the question, and added;

"Because the Delhi office is so extremely unprofessional. There is no work culture here."

PK was too taken aback by the slightly rude tone.

After all Mr. Black Horse was entitled to his own opinion. But PK didn't like the way Mr. Black Horse spoke about the atmosphere in PK's office in Delhi.

****

Mr. Black Horse, PK and one more trainee from the Mumbai office had to spend a few days together at the Client's office in Delhi reviewing agreements, attending meetings and preparing legal reports. PK loved taking time off during weekends but Mr. Black Horse insisted that PK came to office to "finish the work ahead of the deadlines".

The strange thing was that PK was working on weekends all alone. Mr. Black Horse would just not turn up. And PK felt he was "too junior" to ask where his boss was.

Perhaps Mr. Black Horse was attending a meeting somewhere. One day, PK casually checked up from the Client's office about whether Mr. Black Horse was involved in some other meeting somewhere else in Delhi. The official told him that Mr. Black Horse had actually not come to the office. This meant only one thing. His boss was having a great time in Delhi catching up with all his relatives while making PK slog even during the weekends.

****

The "practice" had now become the norm. Mr. Black Horse just did not show up on most of the days. He would come to client meetings late and unprepared. PK had to conduct the meeting with whatever knowledge he had, which was rather limited because this was after all a "Mumbai office case." When Mr.

Black Horse's client asked PK whether there were any legal issues, PK could struggle to point out some which he thought might be of interest to Mr. Black Horse's client. It turned out that everyone was fine with those issues, including Mr. Black Horse.

But in a private meeting, Mr. Black Horse reprimanded PK in front of another trainee from the Mumbai office.

"Look today you caused us so much embarrassment!" Mr. Black Horse admonished.

PK was shocked and confused.

"Why did you point out that legal issue repeatedly in the meeting?" Mr. Black Horse said.

"I thought that issue needed to be addressed if we had to proceed with that corporate transaction," PK replied.

"You could have very well kept your mouth shut. Point a: You didn't speak where you were supposed to speak and point b: Where you were supposed to shut up, you didn't," Mr. Black Horse said sharply, but without making much sense.

PK remained quiet but felt disheartened.

******

Continuing further on the transaction, PK spotted one day a strange error in a document where it said that "the Company in the last 3 years has grown over -3%".

"Minus 3%, how is that possible? Is this a typo or something far more sinister? And which is a typo; -3% or the word 'growth'?" PK thought to himself. As a budding lawyer, he was trained to spot all sorts of potential issues, no matter how silly or strange they looked.

"I have a question to ask, it may sound a little stupid to you but..." PK approached Mr. Black Horse.

Mr. Black Horse was busy punching keys on his laptop. After a few minutes he looked up.

"Show me the document, "Mr. Black Horse said.

PK showed him the -3% line.

"Yes, you have asked a very stupid question. How can it be minus 3% growth?" said Mr. Black Horse and started punching the keys again.

For a moment PK thought that Mr. Black Horse was joking and trying to pull his leg. But Mr. Black Horse didn't show any signs of joking. He was serious.

A little disheartened, PK persisted, "I have some more issues to point out."

"Just write it down in your report and highlight. I'll look at it later," Mr. Black Horse said.

PK did that, for the over 70 agreements and documents that Mr. Black Horse had made PK to review in a few days' time. It was a nearly 100 page report highlighting all issues which PK had spotted so far. PK e-mailed that report to Mr. Black Horse.

No comments came for nearly two weeks. PK also reminded Mr. Black Horse a few times to review his report and to give him feedback, but to no avail.

Every evening PK used to also circulate meeting notes, via e-mail, to everyone (including Mr. Black Horse), clients, his team, the opposite side, etc. Whenever such an email was circulated, PK would invariably receive a reply from Mr. Black Horse pointing out some "mistake" about the font and the font size that was used or something similarly unimportant. There was no comment, however, on any substantial legal issues.

PK's happiness was slowly being sucked away from him like a sponge absorbing excess water.

"May be I make too many mistakes in this profession," PK thought to himself.

On most days, PK would get a call from Mr. Black Horse that he won't be coming to office. A few days before the transaction was going to be completed, Mr. Black Horse called PK for a one-on-one meeting after 6 p.m. He opened PK's 100 page report and saw the highlighted portions.

"THESE ARE VERY SERIOUS LEGAL ISSUES THAT SHOULD HAVE BEEN BROUGHT UP IN MEETINGS WITH OUR CLIENT. WHY HAVE **WE** BEEN SLEEPING ON THIS? WHY DIDN'T YOU TELL ME ABOUT THESE ISSUES BEFORE? I NEED AN EXPLANATION," Mr. Black Horse yelled.

PK was stunned.

"I had tried to point it out but you said that you didn't have time. That's why you asked me to highlight that in a report and email to you," PK tried to explain.

"YOU HAVE BEEN ASKING ALL KINDS OF STUPID QUESTIONS TO ME BUT NOT TAKING THE MOST IMPORTANT ISSUES SERIOUSLY. YOU COULD HAVE BEEN PRO-ACTIVE. YOU COULD HAVE CALLED AND ASKED THE COMPANY OFFICIALS DIRECTLY. I AM NOT GOING TO LISTEN TO ANY MORE EXCUSES. I EXPECTED BETTER WORK ETHICS FROM YOU," Yelled Mr. Black Horse.

PK was now feeling sick. Mr. Black Horse noticed this.

"Hey relax! Calm down. You seem to get stressed out very easily. You should perhaps enrol yourself in a Yoga class," Mr. Black Horse advised.

PK nodded. There was nothing much to say.

Mr. Black Horse first asked PK to get a print out of that 100 page report. Then he made PK sit in front of him while he made changes with a red pen. He then "ordered" PK to make all those changes, that night, sitting in office and hand it over to Mr. Black Horse post-midnight.

PK was fuming internally. Why should he spoil his evening for a work that could have been done a fortnight back? PK was also feeling extremely anxious, tired, depressed, and worn out. He needed to take a break.

So he asked Mr. Black Horse that since he was not feeling too well, could he work on this assignment from home? With a little hesitation, and because he didn't want to do this "menial" work himself, Mr. Black Horse agreed reluctantly.

Just then Mr. Black Horse received a call from his Senior Partner in the Mumbai office lambasting him for "wasting" more than 20 days in Delhi, and asking him to come back immediately. Mr. Black Horse had no option but to comply and so he was off by the next available flight.

The next morning when PK reached office, another Partner (one of PK's super boss in the Delhi office, and popularly referred to as Mr. Blood Sucker) noticed that Mr. Black Horse wasn't hovering around. So he immediately dumped a s**t load of work on PK, not even remotely linked to Mr. Black Horse's project.

Around noon that day, Mr. Black Horse rang up PK from Mumbai, insisting that PK finish the work that day itself. PK told him that it was not possible as he had to now accord priority to his Delhi super boss' work now. PK also wrote an e-mail to Mr. Black Horse explaining this.

As it was going to turn out, it was probably a huge mistake from PK's side.

Mr. Black Horse immediately called PK back and yelled at him. PK tried to explain that this was a rather menial job which could probably be handled by any typist, but to no avail. PK was losing patience now, at being treated as a slave for the Mumbai office. So he decided to hang up and put his phone on the silent mode.

Suddenly an e-mail showed up in PK's mailbox. It was from Mr. Black Horse. The mail was also marked to two Managing Partners (PK's and Mr. Black Horse's Super bosses) from the Delhi and Mumbai office and read:

"I am not able to understand this PK. As mentioned to you earlier, the work required to be done is to revise the summaries prepared by you.

We were to do this on Thursday night but you insisted that you had to go home to which I had said we can do this on Friday morning then. On Friday you probably had taken ill which is fine if you were genuinely unwell and therefore I had not asked you to do any work until you recovered. On Monday noon after we discussed you had stated that you will send in the revised portions by Tuesday morning. Thereafter I receive the following email from you. After this I have been trying to reach you.

I have even left several SMSs to you last night to call me as well. You have not bothered to respond to any of those or call me back. Right now when I got through to your phone you tell me that you haven't returned my call because you have nothing further to add to your email below?! Thereafter again you are not reachable.

I am at a complete loss to understand this. Please let me know by when can I expect the revised summaries.

Mr. Black Horse"

PK was aghast. Mr. Black Horse had surely escalated the matter, with a rather frivolous narration of events as they had transpired. PK could not decide whether he should keep quiet or not. In any case, he needed some time to coolly think over the implications of replying or ignoring.

It was already 7: 30 p.m. in the evening. So PK decided to call it a day and went home. His family members realised that something was not right. PK was not looking like his normal self.

"What's the matter?" PK's father asked him. PK felt deeply embarrassed and didn't say anything. After a while PK opened his laptop and showed the e-mail to his father.

"It is all my fault. My boss thinks that I am a shirker," PK said.

However, PK's father knew in an instant that the matter was NOT really about work, but about power play. Having spent 30 years as a Civil Servant, he knew how bosses operated.

"Son, you need to reply to this e-mail immediately. In corporate bureaucracies all around the world, the one who complains first is heard the loudest. And here Mr. Black Horse has seized the initiative. So this is your opportunity to speak for yourself. Tell your super bosses what you have been through and who is the real culprit," PK's father advised.

PK was stunned. His father was supporting him, instead of criticising him for goofing up.

"But it is not considered right to put the blame on your boss. That will not be acceptable. I won't be regarded as a team player," PK was wavering.

"Who says you are putting the blame on your boss? You are simply telling your version of the story so that your super bosses get a complete picture," PK's father said.

"If you won't stand up for your rights, who else will?" PK's father continued.

"What if I lose my job?" PK said.

"If you won't fight back, you will definitely lose your job. Your super bosses will think that you are the guilty party. A shirker," PK's father said.

"Your boss is a true bully in all sense of the term. Son, always understand that bullies may look very strong but they are actually very weak and shallow from the inside. They thrive on your fear. That is what makes them going. So never succumb to bullying."

This was PK's father's parting advice.

PK agreed hesitatingly. Then he drafted an e-mail. He waited for an hour to chew over things. Then he gave that draft a once over, to ensure that everything looked proper and professional and not like a rant.

PK then sent it off. The e-mail read:

"Dear Mr. Black Horse

If you could kindly recall, I had sent these notes to you a fortnight back. Unfortunately you could not have the time to go through them as you were unable to make it to the office during the Hindu Festival of Ganesh Chaturthi (which I understand was a holiday for you in the Mumbai office but was a working day for us in the Delhi Office). Then on 7th of September 2011, when the bomb blast took place, you told us that as a result of the blast, Central Delhi was sealed and the Delhi Office too would be closed soon. However, we were in the Delhi Office then and continued to work regardless.

Similarly on many such occasions when we were working from the Delhi Office even on a non-working Saturday (such as on 28 August 2011), you continued to remain unavailable for any discussions or consultations. You had also promised then that you would review my notes and send up the mark up by that day itself. Nothing came from your side. On Thursday, when you were supposed to be ready with your comments, by 2 p.m. you had not even started reviewing my notes. Therefore we lost time.

Meanwhile on Monday (12 September) itself, Mr Blood Sucker, Partner (and my super boss) contacted me directly and put me on another matter. I had told you very clearly that I would not, therefore, be able to attend to your work because I was caught up in this assignment. However, when you insisted, to the point of being abusive, I said that I will try my best to send the revision to you by Tuesday morning. When that was not possible, I was forced to inform you that I will not be able to finish your matter.

Regards,

PK"

PK went out for a jog and didn't know what the repercussions were going to be. After half an hour, when he checked his mail, he found his mailbox flooded with e-mails. There was one from Mr. Black Horse where he tried to justify that he never meant to be abusive.

"Really?" PK thought to himself.

Then there were a few e-mails from Mr. Black Horse's Partner, his super boss, asking him to shut up and requesting both him and PK not to shift blame. PK found this e-mail surprising and refreshing.

This Partner then asked PK to get in touch with her directly. PK did that with trembling fingers. But the Partner was like a Fairy God Mother. She listened patiently to all that PK had to say and then asked PK to take his time to complete the assignment and hand it over directly to her without feeling any kind of undue pressure. PK did exactly that and put the episode behind him.

PK could, however, sense that Ms. Fairy God Mother may have received similar complaints about Mr. Black Horse's bullying behaviour from some other sources. Office gossip indicated that his subordinates were taking excessive sick leaves. There was a general drop in performance and motivation in Mr. Black Horse's team while he was busy telling all kinds of stories to Ms. Fairy God Mother about falling standards among the recent recruits. Overall, Mr. Black Horse's conduct was having a negative effect on the performance and consequently the profit margins of the Firm.

The clock was ticking. After a few weeks, every one received a routine mail informing that Mr. Black Horse had "quit to seek better opportunities elsewhere." As everyone knew, this in corporate world is the euphemism for being fired.

Looking back, PK was surprised that he had summoned up some courage to stand up to such a big office bully. His father was even more pleased that his son had retained his wits with him under such tense conditions and had resolved the issue in his own quiet, peaceful way.

"If you're horrible to me, I'm going to write a song about it, and you won't like it. That's how I operate."

— Taylor Swift

(You guessed it right! This is a true story and the protagonist is yours truly, Prasenjeet Kumar or PK.)

5

A Quiet Girl Teaches Bullies A Lesson in Her Own Quiet Way

Sara was a nine year old quiet girl. Her teachers considered her painfully shy, too shy for her own good. Her classmates considered her quietness as "dumbness" or lack of intelligence.

"Why is Sara so quiet?" asked one classmate.

"May be because she has got nothing to say," said another girl.

"May be she is too stupid to say anything," said another classmate laughing out loudly.

Sara was considered like a school blackboard without any writing on it. A Blank Board. She was teased and constantly referred to as Ms. Blank Board.

Sara was quite sensitive to mean comments. She didn't know how to react to the ways her classmates made fun of her. Once Sara tried to reach out to her class teacher but her teacher told her that other children made fun of her because she did not have any friends and that she lacked social skills. She was advised to go out, socialise and befriend her classmates.

Sara tried to do that but nobody wanted to play with Ms. Blank Board. She was deliberately kept out of all gossips and study groups.

"Am I so bad that nobody wants to be friends with me?" Sara brooded.

Depressed and tired of trying to please others, Sara decided that it was best to walk alone and be your own friend. Solitude or as society calls it "loneliness" brings with itself the gifts of freedom and independence. The independence to be yourself, she reasoned.

In her spare time, Sara enjoyed reading fantasy books. The heroic nature of her book's fictional characters fascinated her. She wanted to be like her fictional characters and did not find anyone in her school who was like that, her ideal notion of a friend.

Sara had one more gift that she was not aware of. Her introvert mind had the ability to grasp huge amounts of information, far more than her counterparts. In school she could solve complex mathematical questions in her head.

Sara had one more fascination: chess. She had learnt to move pieces at the age of five. Her father was an avid chess player and very supportive of Sara. He appreciated that his daughter was different, even unique. He realised that Sara was showing some interest in learning chess. So he taught her to play chess in a unique way.

Sara's chess was played without kings or queens, knights or bishops and rooks. Both sides used only pawns to move and to win. The only rule Sara had to follow was that she was supposed to move her pawns beyond the eight rank, overcoming obstacles from the other side, to win. Sara enjoyed the intellectual challenges that the game posed.

Sara loved challenging herself even otherwise. By two, she could solve complex jigsaw puzzles. Before she was four, she could build advanced Lego models that only teenagers could. In her class, Sara knew the flags and population of all the countries in the world. She was indeed gifted with a formidable memory.

While her classmates were busy gossiping about the new girl or boy in school, Sara was reading books on advanced chess theories and could picture moves on a chessboard, all in her mind. This was her new found "gossip magazine". She spent hours reading chess books and didn't stop till she internalised all the moves.

Sara had mastered the history of chess and the moves and tactics of all great players. From a few opening moves, she could identify whether the player was making an *Adams-Huebner* move or a *Kasparov-Fischer* one or some other such chess strategy employed by one of the grandmasters. She even knew the weaknesses of a particular strategy and the ways to effectively deal with it.

Once a boy in Sara's classroom got a chess board and pieces and challenged anyone in the classroom to play chess with him. Soon he found a competitor. Sara was quietly observing the game. To her, the boys looked like complete amateurs. Like a one year old baby learning to walk. The boy's competitor was losing very badly and becoming upset. Sara decided to come to the boy's rescue.

"Look who is coming," said the boy in sarcasm.

Sara offered to help the boy's competitor and told him which pieces to move, in which order. The boy's competitor followed Sara's advice hesitatingly. In a few moves, the competitor could check-mate the other boy. This left the entire class stunned. Ms. Blank Board was showing off her hidden talent. This gave Sara extreme confidence in her ability to become a chess master.

She decided to enrol herself in her school's chess competition. No child could come even close to Sara. She could easily be a Professor of chess at age nine. With every win, Sara became more and more popular in her class. She became the latest gossip, the new found legend. She ultimately went on to win her School's chess championship defeating students who were even four years elder to her. She remained undefeated in all the games she played.

Sara soon became a heroine of her class. Bullies stopped taunting her. Everyone wanted to be friends with her. Any birthday party was considered incomplete without her. Her opinion in group discussions and gossips mattered the most. And even boys started finding her attractive. From a "nobody", Sara became the most talked about girl in school.

This was Sara's quiet way to silence her bullies. Her patience, perseverance and guts to walk all alone by herself paid in the end.

"In order to be open to creativity, one must have the capacity for constructive use of solitude. One must overcome the fear of being alone."

--**Rollo May**

(This story is partly inspired by Magnus Carlsen, who is a Norwegian chess grandmaster, No. 1 ranked player in the world and reigning World Chess Champion in classical, rapid and blitz. His peak rating is 2882, the highest in history.

A chess prodigy, Carlsen became a Grandmaster in 2004, at the age of 13 years, 148 days, making him at that time the second youngest grandmaster in history. On 1 January 2010, at the age of 19 years, 32 days, he became the youngest chess player in history to be ranked world No. 1. In November 2013, Carlsen defeated Viswanathan Anand in the World Chess Championship 2013, thus becoming the new world chess champion, and subsequently defended his title during the World Chess Championship 2014 in November 2014 defeating Anand again.)

6

A "Quiet dull witted child" becomes an immortal scientist

Al was a calm, dreamy, slow, but self-assured and determined child. The biggest problem in his childhood was his "quietness." He was slow in learning to speak; so slow that his parents thought that their son had a speech disability and even consulted a doctor. At the age of seven, Al used to repeat his sentences to himself or in other words "talked to himself." This made friends, neighbours, family members and relatives wonder whether Al was somewhat dim-witted.

In school, Al had trouble adjusting to the conventional teaching methods. He did not like the fact that schools promoted a mind-set of unquestionable obedience and senseless discipline. Al was slow in giving "quick automated responses," a criterion that teachers used to evaluate the talent and 'worthiness' of students. Al was never considered an ideal student. One teacher was even nasty enough to tell Al that he would never get anywhere in life!

Nevertheless, Al had his own world. He loved solitude. Numbers and musical notes filled his Universe. While his peers played in the ground, Al solved arithmetical problems and played the violin. Some psychologists even wondered whether Al was dyslexic, autistic or even schizophrenic.

However, Al had certain gifts from God that nobody else had; an amazing knack for self-learning and concentration. By age 12, Al had a fondness for solving complicated problems in applied arithmetic. He believed that he could jump ahead the school curriculum and learn geometry and algebra on his own. His parents were kind and supportive enough to buy him the textbooks in advance so that he could master them over the summer vacations. Not only did Al learn the proofs in the books, he also attempted to prove the new theories on his own. He even came up with his own way to prove the Pythagorean theorem.

By age 15, Al was solving complex mathematical equations that nobody could, including his teachers. In class, he always scored top marks. Yet he was considered as a *"brilliant underachiever"* by his teachers.

Al also had another phenomenal ability, an ability which could make him immortal. That was his ability to think in terms of pictures rather than words. How strange, one might ask!

This meant that Al could perform visual experiments in his head rather than in the lab. Have you ever imagined yourself riding alongside a light beam? How would the light waves appear to you? Would the light beams appear stationary to you, if you were travelling at the same speed as that of light; something which commonly happens if two trains are running on parallel tracks at the same speed and you happen to sit in one of them?

This is exactly what Al pictured in his mind when he was only 16 years old.

In another instance, Al imagined a lightning bolt striking the two ends of a moving train. How would you see the lightning strike if you were standing on an embankment? Won't you see the strikes hitting the train simultaneously?

Now, what if you were sitting inside the train? Would you still see the strikes hitting the train simultaneously? Probably not. You would see it as happening in two different moments.

So how you see things, Al theorised, depends upon where you were standing or sitting and your state of motion i.e. your perception is relative.

A ground breaking scientific discovery was about to be made. Al realised that there is no such thing as an absolute time. Time is relative. Al's over-active imagination led to the birth of the-then unheard 'Theory of relativity.'

I'm sure you would have guessed by now who is Al in our story.

Yes, it is the noted physicist **Albert Einstein**.

In 1921, Einstein became the recipient of the Nobel Prize, "for his services to theoretical physics, and especially for his discovery of the law of the photoelectric effect."

His scientific theories, quantum theory and relativity, had a profound impact not only on the way we view science but also on philosophy and morality. Scientists still uphold his theories and he has become very much a part and parcel of our culture.

But did you know that Einstein demonstrated the classic strengths of an introvert? Introverts have a knack for self-learning and so did Einstein. He learnt geometry and algebra on his own.

Introverts are supposed to have a rich inner world. Einstein had one too. His rich inner world led him to discover relativity. Most importantly, Einstein utilised his power of concentration (which is another gift of being quiet) to make stellar progress.

Lots of rumour float around Einstein that he was dyslexic, suffered from learning disability, was mildly autistic or even schizophrenic. However, these rumours have been dismissed as baseless. Einstein had the ability to pick up new languages and learn violin and many scientific disciplines on his own. So there was no question of any kind of learning disability.

A person is considered autistic if he is socially withdrawn, lacks empathy for peers and cannot have a normal social relationship with others. Einstein could make friends in school and college and had empathy for his peers. His 'problem; was that he preferred to work in solitude but that didn't make him autistic.

"The true sign of intelligence is not knowledge but imagination."

--Albert Einstein

7

Lessons that all introvert entrepreneurs can learn

There is a popular myth that introverts cannot be as successful as their extroverted counterparts when it comes to entrepreneurship or rising to the Executive Level. Introverts are slow in decision making and attending too many conferences and meetings drain them out. Yet there are so many successful introvert entrepreneurs ranging from Bill Gates to Mark Zuckerberg.

How is that possible?

Introverts have their own superpowers which if they harness properly can make them rise to the top. There is no better example to demonstrate this than the story of a boy who was born in 1901 in Chicago, Illinois.

This boy had a troubled childhood. His father was abusive and believed in corporal punishment so much so that this boy's brothers ran away from home. The boy, like a typical introvert, lived in a world of his own. His world comprised of drawings, cartoons, animations and sketches. From the age of four, he was drawing and selling cartoons to his neighbours. His father dismissed his boy's talent simply as a childhood fantasy that could never ever fully support him.

In his young adult years, the boy was bold enough to drop out of high school to pursue a career in animation. Briefly, he also worked with a newspaper agency and was fired for his *"lack of imagination and ideas."*

One fine morning, on a train ride from New York, the boy, now a man, came up with a sketch of a giant mouse wearing shorts which he thought had a real potential to be a popular animated cartoon character. No bank was willing to fund his project because they thought that the idea was absurd. Nearly 300 banks rejected his project but that did not stop the man from pursuing his mission.

Did the story ring a bell somewhere?

Which man would have the guts to continue after suffering 300 rejections?

You would, if you were Walt Disney and if the mouse cartoon character, which you would have correctly guessed by now, was Mickey Mouse.

"All our dreams can come true, if we have the courage to pursue them," said Walt Disney. He was met with failure after failure yet he never gave up. Like a classic introvert, Walt Disney, believed in persistence.

Walt Disney first formed his animation Company in Kansas City in 1921. However, issues with unscrupulous distributors led to the Company being dissolved and Disney being left without the money to even pay for rent or food. He was forced to leave for Los Angeles with only $40 in cash, and a suitcase containing only a shirt, two undershorts, two pairs of socks and some drawing materials.

In 1927 Walt Disney and his team created a character known as "Oswald the Lucky Rabbit," but a clause in Disney's contract led to his distributors owning all the rights to this cartoon character. A common phenomena in the artistic world. No credit was given to Walt Disney. His distributors even "stole" Disney's staff except for his friend Ub Iwerks. Disney was devastated but declared that *"never again will I work for somebody else."*

As a successful entrepreneur, Walt Disney learnt from his mistakes. By the time his new character Mickey Mouse was launched, he made sure that he owned all the rights for his cartoon characters.

"A giant mouse on the screen would terrify women," was the reaction of MGM studios when Walt approached them to distribute Mickey Mouse in 1927. Today Mickey Mouse is a billion dollar brand. Truly Disney's formidable career was all sparked off by a mouse.

In the 1940s, Pinocchio became an extremely expensive venture. Disney poured millions of dollars to reshape the story and add special effects and sound. In the end, Pinocchio lost millions of dollars after its first release.

In 1942, Bambi was released. The most powerful and un-forgetful scene where Bambi's mother was shot was considered amusing by the audience. Walt had to conclude that the Second World War era was probably not the correct time to launch a movie about deer love.

On the personal front, Walt had to suffer from fits of anger, immense frustration, and depression. There were times when his future looked extremely bleak and uncertain. Yet Disney had a vision. That vision led to the creation of Disneyland.

Disney had a dysfunctional relationship with his father yet he was determined to create 'the happiest place on earth' for parents and children. It took him nearly seven years to complete his project, whereas most people would have given up after a year. He later went on to create water parks, hotels and resorts. Disney was always focussed on the bigger picture.

Walt Disney once admitted that he was *"scared to death"* when he had to face the camera to introduce episodes of the "Disneyland" television series. However, nothing could stop Disney from pursuing his ambitions. Disney had seen everything in his career: poverty, depression, stolen ideas, death of his beloved mother, inventions that were mocked at, et al.

Disney went on to win a total of twenty-six Academy Awards, and holds the record for most Academy Awards in history. He received twenty-two competitive Academy Awards from a total of fifty-nine nominations. Disney also holds the records for most wins and most nominations for an individual in history.

Sadly Walt Disney died in 1966 due to lung cancer but his corporation is billion dollars' worth and is still a rolling giant that can't be trifled with.

Disney proved that any successful entrepreneur should have three characteristics: vision, ability to learn from past mistakes and a never give up attitude even under the most trying circumstances.

"It's kind of fun to do the impossible"

– Walt Disney

III

Living Your Dreams

Are you unhappy with your current job?

Do you feel that your job is too high pressured or not in accordance with your temperament?

What if you lost your job but don't know whether you should see it as a curse or a blessing?

In this final part, I bring you a story about an introvert changing her career in accordance with her temperament. Please don't take this story as an advice for career change.

8

Which is more important: Happiness and Love or Money and Stress?

Martha joined the Marketing division of a small company. The job sounded like a lucrative profession with decent salary and perks. Martha initially thought that the job was a perfect fit for her.

However, there was one problem. The job was not in sync with her introvert personality. The profession rewarded those who spoke first and fast, were loud, aggressive and the ones who always took the centre stage.

Martha worked quietly behind the scenes and was not even regarded a team-player, whatever that may mean. She also had to work with abusive bosses and was constantly subjected to tirades, name calling and threats of being fired. The profession was slowly killing Martha day by day.

Once an enthusiastic worker, Martha now used to have tears in her eyes while leaving for office on the Monday morning. She tried to speak to her colleagues regarding her abusive boss but was advised to put up with such kind of behaviour.

"Your boss is loud but he doesn't mean it. He is one of the most experienced people in the industry and I am sure you will learn a lot from him in the longer run," advised one of Martha's colleagues.

"Well this is how the industry operates. It is part of disciplining employees. And it is still better than the s**t that happens in other places," commiserated another.

"Why don't you quit your job and find something else that suits your nature," suggested the third one.

Martha didn't know what to do or whom to listen to. After 12-14 hours of work per day, she had difficulty sleeping in the night. While travelling to work, she used to feel dizzy or light headed. Her hands would tremble while speaking to her bosses and colleagues which sort of embarrassed her. She was having terrible back aches. Martha felt drained. In her college days, she enjoyed jogging but now she felt exhausted all the time. Martha didn't realise that she was showing the first signs of a nervous breakdown.

"What if my boss fired me?" Martha kept thinking to herself.

Then the day came when Martha's fear actually came to be true. She was asked to go and find another job. Martha felt relieved a little that she did not need to deal with her abusive bosses anymore but she was also worried about her future.

While receiving unemployment benefits, Martha wanted to take some time off. She had heard about the wonderful benefits of yoga in stress management and wanted to give it a try. She joined a Yoga centre and soon learnt various poses, breathing exercises and mediation. Yoga not only helped her improve her flexibility, balance and back muscles but the mediation exercises made her understand her true self.

Martha realised that she was not made for the corporate jungle where the survival of only the most vocal, loud, aggressive and the pushy was guaranteed. Life was too short for that. She also realised that her life mission was to help and care for others facing health and mental issues. Her purpose now was to help those who were like her trapped in employment and facing issues of nervous breakdown, sleepless nights, and back aches. Yoga had opened up a new possibility for her. Her new career was awaiting her.

Martha now wanted to be a Yoga teacher. She completed 200 hours of training to certify as a Yoga teacher. She realised that it was easier to get a job in a smaller town than in a big cosmopolitan city. So she left for a small town located in the mountains with green pastures, snow peaks, red roses and blue lakes. There Martha started teaching yoga to her students.

Life was not easy. Martha had to live in a small apartment, sell her TV and cut out on eating out. Yet Martha was happy doing what she was doing. She did not now have sleepless nights. Her trembling was gone forever. Her back aches disappeared and she felt fit like she never had. Mentally she was far more at peace with herself.

"What was the point of a highly paid job if it was only going to pay for your future medical bills and that too when the cause of your health problem was the job itself?" Martha wondered.

Yoga invoked her creative side and now she was focussing more on connecting with people and listening to her heart. Her students loved her.

Martha feels that a time will come when money too will follow.

And that money will come not from tyrannising junior employees but from the love and deep care that she has for others.

A Big Thank You!

Thank you so much for purchasing my book.

I know that you could have picked up any other book on this subject but you took a chance with mine.

A big thanks also for reading my book all the way to the end.

I'm obliged.

If you liked this book, I shall be grateful if you could do me a small favour by taking a moment to leave a review on Amazon.

Your feedback is of immense value to me as an Author. Your suggestions will help me in writing the kind of books that you love.

FREE GIFT

As a way of saying thanks for your purchase, I'm offering FREE the first few chapters of my first book in the series **Quiet Phoenix: An Introvert's Guide to Rising in Career & Life**.

This excerpt is bigger and more detailed than the one you will find on Amazon, should you choose to preview my book. You may download the excerpt from here:

http://eepurl.com/_-WUL

Do You Also Want To Write A Book?

I am sure that you too would have an interesting story to tell the world, just as I did in this book.

I believe that writing a book can truly heal you.

But did you know that you can easily self-publish your book and make it available to readers worldwide in almost 100 countries within 12-48 hours of your writing?

Yes, you read it correctly.

You do not need to bang the doors of a traditional publisher anymore till your book is accepted, even though you can still follow that route, if you so wish.

I constantly share tips about self-publishing including how to write books, proof read and edit them, design their covers, format and market them and much more at http://www.publishwithprasen.com

If you want a book to help jump-start your career with self-publishing, you may like to download this FREE Report "If I could publish, without spending a dime, 3 books, in six months, so can you..." here:

http://eepurl.com/_pc_D

This FREE REPORT contains almost everything you need to know about self-publishing. It also has a helpful list of video tutorials and books that you can refer to at your leisure to gain more skills.

You can also contact me at prasenjeet@publishwithprasen.com or tweet me @PublishWithPras

Acknowledgment

To my dear mother and father for their unflinching support and belief in my abilities without which I couldn't have written this book.

Disclaimer

The Author has tried to recreate, wherever relevant, events, locales and conversations from his memories of them. In order to maintain their anonymity in some instances, the Author has changed the names of individuals and places, including some identifying characteristics and details such as physical properties, occupations and places of residence.

Other Books by the Author

QUIET PHOENIX: AN INTROVERT'S GUIDE TO RISING IN CAREER & LIFE

Amazon #1 Best Seller in Legal Profession and Ethics and Professional Responsibility

Awaken the Phoenix Bird inside You.

Rise in Your Career. Love Your Profession.

In a first-of-its-kind tell-all memoir on the inside working of a top Indian law firm, corporate lawyer turned author Prasenjeet Kumar, shares his experiences in as candid and no-holds-barred manner as never disclosed in this genre before.

This makes "Quiet Phoenix" an invaluable, 242 pages, book:

First, for all law students who have starry eyed notions of working in a corporate law firm;

Second, for those Junior Associates who have just entered the portals of their dream firm and are bewildered, for example, at the senselessly long hours they are required to clock in; and

Third, for the Managing Partners who need to see in the mirror how horrible they look and what they need to do to become human again.

With extensive research and penetrating insight, the book also focuses on the "problems" of introverts who feel that:

Their extroverted colleagues are better at marketing themselves and in getting ahead in career;

They feel sick and tired of long working hours;

They don't know how to deal with office bullies;

They are aghast at Co-workers stealing their ideas;

They can't believe that their bosses can practice blatant favouritism;

Or that they can have a Colleague just round the corner who is willing to back stab them without any provocation.

Using everyday office incidents, experiences and politics that anyone (and not just lawyers) can immediately relate to, "Quiet Phoenix" not only inspires but makes you come with your own uniquely actionable plan.

The characters used in the book are so life-like that they will immediately remind you of someone in your office.

You have the Senior Associate one Mr. Late Nightaholic who loves to let his juniors twiddle their thumbs the whole day and then at 06.30 pm dumps a lot of work to keep them busy the whole night.

Then you have Ms. Senior Partner, who despite being a junior associate acts as she is the senior partner for all junior associates.

Next is Ms. Goof-up Queen, who is trying to be a senior associate by proving that she is the only one NOT goofing up while everyone around her is churning out sheer garbage.

And at the very top is the partner Mr. Blood Sucker who is where he is because he is a childhood chum of the owner of the firm.

Like the legendary Phoenix bird rising from the ashes "Quiet Phoenix" is meant to specifically help all introverts or Quiet persons to lift them up literally from the bootstraps, by constantly reminding them that introversion is NOT a handicap to be ashamed of. In fact, Introverts are supposed to have amazing powers of concentration, engaged listening, and an ability to foster deep relationships with friends and clients.

Over all, "Quiet Phoenix" is an incredible story that Prasenjeet Kumar shares, with wit and charm, of the journey from being a Corporate Lawyer to becoming a Full Time Author-Entrepreneur using his introversion as strength to overcome all obstacles.

QUIET PHOENIX 2: FROM FAILURE TO FULFILMENT: A MEMOIR OF AN INTROVERTED CHILD

Amazon #1 Hot New Releases in Biographies & Memoirs > Professional and Academics > Educators

Celebrating The Quiet Child: A Must Read For every Parent, Teacher, Mentor, Sports Coach........

From Prasenjeet Kumar, the author of Quiet Phoenix, the Amazon #1 Bestseller in the Hot New Releases category, comes a sequel that no one who deals with introverted children should miss.

The underlying theme of the book is that just as a Phoenix Bird is hardwired to be reborn from the ashes of her ancestors, her tears are meant to cure wounds and she symbolises undying hope and optimism, so is your Quiet child built for persistence, creativity, and self-discipline; and for displaying a knack for self-learning, high emotional intelligence and an impeccable sense of moral responsibility.

Instead of cherishing such rare traits

Introverts are sadly often misunderstood by almost every one.

Parents worry if their children prefer spending time in solitude, probably day dreaming.

Teachers presume that if a child hesitates to answer questions, she must be having some kind of learning or even social disability.

Quiet Children have difficulties in making friends, with their classmates seeing them as "weird", "rude" or "arrogant".

They are seen as "over" sensitive to mean comments or bullying.

They appear to lack aggression or as some say 'the will to fight back'.

Overall, introverted children seem to be more flustered about almost every facet of life in noisy and large Public Schools.

Any advice that Quiet children should be more 'outgoing', 'sociable' and 'active' seems to be counterproductive.

Any aggressive follow up on this advice often results in your Quiet child losing her self-esteem, forcing her to become even more withdrawn.

With fables, stories and real incidents from the author's own childhood "Quiet Phoenix 2: From Failure to Fulfilment"

Reiterates that introvert Children being asked to behave in a more extroverted fashion is like asking a young Phoenix bird to behave like an Eagle.

Every child is born with some unique traits. The challenge is: how parents, teachers and friends can recognize, nurture and enhance those powers so that every child, quiet or loquacious, becomes a winner.

"Quiet Phoenix 2: From Failure to Fulfilment" sincerely intends to help everyone dealing with 'Quiet Children' to cherish and celebrate them for what they are.

And to help them rise above everything; to lead them towards a path of happiness leaving behind all old memories of pain and isolation; and to turn them into life's winners.

Just like the Phoenix rising from the ashes.

With real life characters like Ms. Brownie Points, Mr. Noisy Ferrari and Ms. Pencil Snatcher, this book is intended for everyone--a parent, teacher, or sports Coach..

Who wants to understand how to harness the powers of Quiet children in an extroverted world.

And if you are an introvert adult, you may find this book useful in understanding yourself, your past and what you want out of life in the future.

So what are you waiting for?

Books By The Author in Other Genres

(Based on the recipes of Sonali Kumar, Author's mom)

HOW TO CREATE A COMPLETE MEAL IN A JIFFY

Presenting a Cookbook Like No Other Cookbook in the World

From the popular website www.cookinginajiffy.com and the author of four Amazon Bestseller cookbooks comes a cookbook that doesn't focus on recipes.

Instead, it shares the secret of creating a Full Meal in around 30 minutes.

How is that possible?

With just Proper Sequencing and Parallel Processing of your actions, is author Prasenjeet Kumar's answer.

So if till now you didn't know (or hadn't thought about) as to how with proper sequencing and parallel processing you can reduce your drudgery by many, many fold, you have come absolutely to the right place.

In that background, the Book presents around 40 dishes grouped into 10 Full Meals consisting of: two "concepts" of breakfasts, four Indian meals, one Thai meal, one Japanese meal, and two Western meals.

HOME STYLE INDIAN COOKING IN A JIFFY

Amazon #1 Best Seller in Indian Cooking and Professional Cooking

With an amazing compilation of over 100 delectable Indian dishes, many of which you can't get in any Indian restaurant for love or for money, this is unlike any other Indian Cook book. What this book focuses on is what Indians eat every day in their homes. It then in a step-by-step manner makes this mysterious, never disclosed, "Home Style" Indian cooking accessible to anyone with a rudimentary knowledge of cooking and a stomach for adventure.

Prasenjeet Kumar, the corporate lawyer turned gourmand, in this second book of his series "How to Cook everything in a Jiffy" explores the contours of what sets Indian "Home Style" food so apart from restaurant food. In his uniquely semi-autobiographical style, he starts with his quest for

Indian food in London, wonders why his European friends don't have such a "strange" debate between "Home Style" and "Restaurant" food, and learns that the whole style of restaurant cooking in India is diametrically opposed to what is practiced in Indian homes with respect to the same dish.

You may like this book if:

You are an Indian pining for a taste of your home food anywhere in the world, including India.

You are an Indian, reasonably adept in your own regional cuisine, for example, South Indian cuisine, but want to learn about the "Home Style" culinary traditions of the Eastern and Northern India as well.

You are NOT an Indian but you love Indian cuisine and have wondered if someone could guide you through the maze of spices that Indians use, and help you tame down the oil and chilli levels of many of their dishes.

Recommends Amazon.com Top 100 Reviewer Mysterious Reviewer "There's plenty to like concerning the Home Style Indian Cooking In a Jiffy cookbook by author Prasenjeet Kumar. Kumar has formatted the book so each recipe links back to the interactive table of contents making navigation easy. He's also included color photos illustrating his recipe throughout his cookbook. Best of all Kumar offers information how to set up a basic kitchen, a brief introduction to Indian spices and goes onto offer various chapters covering Indian food.

His recipes offer both the standard cooking method or the option to use a pressure cooker (when appropriate) to prepare the recipe. He gives clear directions how to complete the task using either cooking method..."

HOW TO COOK IN A JIFFY EVEN IF YOU HAVE NEVER BOILED AN EGG BEFORE

Amazon Top 5 Best Seller in Cooking for One

Introducing "How To Cook In A Jiffy"— The Easiest Cookbook On Earth From The Author Of The Hugely Popular Website www.cookinginajiffy.com

Never boiled an egg before but want to learn the magic art of cooking? Then don't leave home without this Survival Cookbook. Be it healthy college cooking, or cooking for a single person or even outdoor cooking---this easiest cookbook on earth teaches you to survive all situations with ease.

Where this book scores over other "How To" cookbooks is the structured manner in which it follows a step by step "graduation" process.

Most uniquely, the book teaches the concept of "sequencing and parallel processing" in cooking to enable busy people to create a 3-4 course meal in less than 30 minutes.

The book is fun and entertaining to read with the author sharing his own personal story of bumbling about in the wonderlands of cooking, with wit and humour.

Recommends Amazon.com reviewer B. Farrell "This is a good informative book for someone starting out in the adventure of cooking. This would make a great gift for a young bride just starting out with her new duties of cooking or a single person getting out on their own."

HEALTHY COOKING IN A JIFFY: THE COMPLETE NO FAD NO DIET HANDBOOK

Amazon #1 in Hot New Releases in Health, Fitness & Dieting> Special Diets> Healthy

Amazon #3 Best Seller in Health, Fitness & Dieting> Special Diets> Healthy

If you have ever wondered how you can be healthy without dieting, following any peculiar fads, eating any esoteric foods, injecting any hormones or downing any pills, potions or supplements, you have come absolutely to the right place.

In fact, without bothering about the risk of sounding so old fashioned, author Prasenjeet Kumar (of the celebrated website cookinginajiffy.com and the writer of the "How to Cook Everything in a Jiffy" series of cookbooks) declares that he does not think that anyone should be on a perpetual diet to stay healthy. In this book, therefore, he recommends that you do not follow any of the rather peculiar diet regimes such as a low carb high protein diet, low fat diet, Vegan diet (unless you truly believe in the vegan philosophy) or any kind of crash diets. From his own experience, he says that that they will all do you more harm than good.

Instead, the author recommends going to the basics that of following a balanced diet regime. In that background, the book presents a veritable cornucopia of easy recipes to give you an idea of what you can cook to achieve your target of having regularly a balanced diet. You will find ideas on how to cook your vegetables in a simple and tasty manner, how to handle pasta recipes, chicken recipes, fish recipes, mutton recipes, milk shakes (even if you hate drinking plain milk), breakfast recipes, lunch and dinner recipes and some Asian recipes when you feel the need to have something different and exciting.

Surprisingly, you will find some supposedly "unhealthy" recipes as waffles, pancakes, French toasts, lasagne and lamb moussaka too in this "healthy" cookbook. The author's short answer is, that the wonderful taste of these dishes makes you happy and being happy (and full of serotonin) is more than half way to being healthy. Moreover, as the author believes, any sensible person will have these dishes only once-in-a-while when you are bored eating your regular stuff.

Again, quite boldly, the author declares that personally he does not count calories in his diet, oops recipes. He feels that counting calories can actually drive you mad. This book celebrates exactly this very viewpoint and deliberately with some justifiable pride eschews providing any calorific or nutritional information for the listed recipes. If you want to still count calories, feel free to do so by taking advantage of so many tools that are readily available on the internet, the author advises.

At the end of this book, there are tips relating to how you can manage to have five to six small meals a day, regardless of your busy schedule, how you can exercise even if you are not a "gym person", how to freeze and preserve leftovers and finally how to sequence and parallel process your actions so that you save time while cooking your meals.

So if you are sick of dieting, counting calories, or gorging on supplements, do consider investing in this book of simply sensible cooking and get on to a journey of eternal joy and happiness.

THE ULTIMATE GUIDE TO COOKING LENTILS THE INDIAN WAY

Amazon #1 Best Seller in Rice & Grains

Presenting 58 Tastiest Ways to Cook Lentils as Soups, Curries, Snacks, Full Meals and hold your breath, Desserts! As only Indians can.

From the author of # 1 Amazon Best seller "Home Style Indian Cooking In A Jiffy"

This is simply the ultimate vegetarian protein cookbook.

We all know that as the cheapest and most versatile sources of protein available to mankind, lentils have been cultivated and consumed from the time immemorial.

Lentils are mentioned in religious books such as the Bible, Quran and the Vedas.

Lentils were so important for those long sea voyages that the Romans named their emperors after the most common legumes: Lentulus (lentil), Fabius (fava), Piso (pea), and Cicero (chickpea).

And yet, lentils came to be almost forgotten in the modern post-20th century world with easy availability of red meat and the rise of fast food joints.

Now thanks to scientists and expert bodies like the Mayo Clinic, we know that lentils are actually better than meat.

Lentils are actually the "Healthiest Food" in the World.

Lentils are good for a Healthy Heart: Lentils contain significant amount of folate and magnesium, both doing wonders for your heart.

Lentils replenish Iron Needed for Energy: Lentils are rich in Iron, which is a vital component of energy production and metabolism in the body.

Lentils are low in cholesterol: Lentils, unlike red meat, are low in fat, calories and cholesterol. They are also somewhat lower in oxalic acid and similar chemicals which cause stone formation in kidneys and result in gout, a painful affliction of joints caused by the deposition of crystals.

Lentils are rich in fibre: If you are looking for ways to reduce constipation, try Lentils as they contain a high amount of dietary fibre, both soluble and insoluble.

The way Indians cook lentils is unmatched by any other cuisine on Planet Earth.

No one can cook lentils the way Indians do.

This is because almost every Indian meal has to have a lentil dish, as dal (soup), curry, snack or dessert. So they have centuries of expertise in turning lentils in whichever way you want.

On the other hand, most western cook books would, at the most, recommend baking lentils with cheese, putting them in hamburgers, having them with sausages and casseroles or making lentils stew.

One is, of course, not counting the lentils sprouts salad or the famous students' dorm dish of baked beans (straight from the can) as well as the West

Asian "sauce" hummus, without which no Lebanese meal can be termed complete.

There is nothing wrong if you want to have your lentils this way.

But if you want to experiment, and wish to embark upon a roller coaster culinary adventure, you must look at Indian cuisine.

"**The Ultimate Guide to Cooking Lentils the Indian Way**" lets you savour, in this background, as many as twenty most popular "Home Style" dal recipes; ten curries; six lentil dishes cooked with rice; eleven snacks; three kebabs; three lentil stuffed parathas; and five desserts.

It is said that without carrying Sattu or roasted chickpea flour with them, for sustenance on those long and arduous treks, Buddhist monks from Bihar could NOT have spread Buddhism to far off places from Afghanistan and Tibet to Korea!

Still don't believe about India's robust lentil tradition?

Connect with Me

I would love to connect with you on Social Media. Join me on:

Facebook:

https://www.facebook.com/prasenjeet.kumar.925

Twitter: https://twitter.com/PublishWithPras

Google Plus:

https://www.google.com/+PrasenjeetKumarAuthor

Goodreads:

https://www.goodreads.com/prasenjeet

About the Author

Prasenjeet Kumar is a Law graduate from the University College London (2005-2008), London University and a Philosophy Honours graduate from St. Stephen's College (2002-2005), Delhi University. In addition, he holds a Legal Practice Course (LPC) Diploma from College of Law, Bloomsbury, London.

Prasenjeet loves gourmet food, music, films, golf and travelling. He has already covered seventeen countries including Canada, China, Denmark, Dubai, Germany, Hong Kong, Indonesia, Macau, Malaysia, Sharjah, Sweden, Switzerland, Thailand, Turkey, UK, Uzbekistan, and the USA.

Prasenjeet is the self-taught designer, writer, editor and proud owner of the website http://www.cookinginajiffy.com/which he has dedicated to his mother and http://www.publishwithprasen.com where he shares tips on self- publishing.

Printed in Poland
by Amazon Fulfillment
Poland Sp. z o.o., Wrocław